The Heroines of History

★ ★ ★ ★ ★ ★

Heroines of the American Revolution

AMERICA'S FOUNDING MOTHERS

The Heroines of History

★ ★ ★ ★ ★ ★

Heroines of the American Revolution

AMERICA'S FOUNDING MOTHERS

★ ★ ★ ★ ★ ★

by Diane Silcox-Jarrett

Illustrations by Art Seiden

SCHOLASTIC INC.

New York Toronto London Auckland Sydney
Mexico City New Delhi Hong Kong

Dedication

To Daniel and Kimberly. May you always be
interested in those who have come before you.

ISBN 0-439-25947-9

12 11 10 9 8 7 6 5   3 4 5/0

Printed in the U.S.A.   14

First Scholastic printing, October 2000

Book design by Arvid Knudsen & Associates
Edited by Ellen E.M. Roberts
Electronic composition by DAK Graphics

Contents

Introduction by Sylvia Hoffert, Ph.D. / 4
American Revolutionary War Events / 6
The American Colonies in the 1770's / 7

Abigail Adams: Champion for Equal Rights for Women / 9
Hannah Arnett: The Patriot Wife Who Would Not Be Quiet / 12
Penelope Barker: Leader of the Edenton Tea Party / 15
Catherine Moore Barry: The Heroine of Cowpens / 18
Martha Bratton: A Brave and Compassionate Patriot Woman / 20
Elizabeth Burgin: Organizer of the Great Prisoner Escape / 24
Margaret Corbin: Captain Molly / 29
Lydia Darragh: Quaker Woman of Conscience / 32
Emily Geiger: The Quick–Thinking Messenger / 36
Nancy Hart: The War Woman of Broad River / 39
Sybil Ludington: The Female Paul Revere / 42
Grace and Rachel Martin: Interceptors of the Courier / 45
Molly Hays McCauley: Molly Pitcher / 49
Rebecca Motte: The Patriot Who Burned Her Home / 53
Mary Lindley Murray: The Woman Who Stopped the British Army / 56
Esther Reed: Organizer of the Philadelphia Association / 59
Betsy Ross: Making the Flag / 62
Deborah Sampson: Patriot Soldier Disguised as a Man / 63
Nancy Ward: Beloved Woman of the Cherokee / 67
Mercy Otis Warren: Patriot Playwright / 70
Phillis Wheatley: The First African-American Author / 75
Patience Wright: American Spy in King George's Court / 78
Prudence Wright: Commander of the Minutewomen / 82
Elizabeth Zane: The Heroine of Fort Henry / 86

Index / 90
About the Author / 92
About the Artist / 92

Introduction

When the American Revolution started in 1775, most colonists lived on farms and in small towns. White women spent most of their time at home. Their daughters had to work hard because things we buy at the store were made at home. They helped their mothers to spin and weave cloth and sew clothes. They made soap for washing, churned butter, and cooked every meal. They fed the chickens and the pigs. They worked in the garden to raise vegetables and herbs.

Women were valued for their work, not for their intelligence. Some boys went to school but most girls had to stay at home. Girls rarely learned to read and write.

When a girl grew up, she was free to marry whomever she wanted. But if she chose the wrong man, she was probably stuck for life. If her husband treated her badly, she couldn't do anything about it. And if that were not bad enough, her husband controlled all her property. He could take her land, clothes and jewelry and give them away. There was little a wife could do to stop him.

Children were important in colonial households. Women usually had a baby every two years. Families in the American colonies were much larger than they are today. But many children died when they were babies. So taking care of children, who were often sick, kept women very busy.

Before the American Revolution, women could not vote or hold office. They listened while their husbands talked about why they were mad at King George. Many housewives agreed that they should not have to pay high taxes. They agreed with their husbands that it wasn't fair that they had no representatives in Parliament. They were angry when forced to feed and house British soldiers.

The Sons of Liberty asked women to stop buying British tea in order to show how mad they were. So women had to think about whether or not they wanted to use their buying power to support the Patriot cause. Some women decided that they did not want to and became Loyalists. Others did what they could to support independence and drive out the British. American women had begun to think about political issues and choose sides.

The first of the American Revolution battles took place on the road between Lexington and Concord. Afterwards the British marched away to Boston. George Washington and his army surrounded them. Eventually, the Americans forced the

British to leave Boston and flee to Canada. But shortly after the Declaration of Independence was signed in 1776, the British came back and took New York City. Then they moved to Philadelphia. Washington's army spent a miserable winter nearby at Valley Forge. They suffered from hunger and freezing temperatures. By spring, they were able to drive the British out of Philadelphia.

The British could not defeat the colonists in the north. So they moved their army farther south. By 1780, even the women in the Carolinas and Georgia had to worry about what the British soldiers might be doing in their area.

The last battle of the war was the battle of Yorktown. The Americans trapped the British and forced them to give up. After the battle, the lives of most American women returned to normal. They remained housewives and mothers. Their husbands continued to control women's property. American men were glad that their wives and daughters had supported the Patriot cause. Nonetheless, they still refused to give women the right to vote and hold office.

It took many years for things to change. The American Revolution had shown that no government could last unless women supported it. Men began to believe that mothers should be responsible for training their children to be hard working and patriotic citizens. To do so, women needed a better education. So girls were sent to school to learn to read and write and think.

But when they began to think for themselves, women realized that they still were not being treated the same way as men. Women began to fight for their own rights. They demanded the right to control their own property. They demanded the right to vote and hold office. Finally after many years they got the rights they wanted. The struggle to make sure that men and women are treated as equals is still going on today.

Stories about the American Revolution are usually about battles, generals, and soldiers. Most women were not soldiers and did not fight in battles. But they did contribute to the struggle for American freedom. This book about revolutionary heroines is an important reminder to young people that women's patriotism and bravery helped to win American independence.

Sylvia D. Hoffert Ph.D.
Professor of History
University of North Carolina — Chapel Hill

American Revolutionary War Events

1765	British Parliament passes the Stamp Act.
1766	British Parliament repeals the Stamp Act.
1767	Parliament passes Townsend Duties taxing tea.
March 5, 1770	Boston Massacre.
December 16, 1773	Boston Tea Party.
September 5, 1774	First meeting of the Continental Congress.
April 19, 1775	Battle of Lexington and Concord.
June 17, 1775	Battle of Bunker Hill and Breed's Hill.
January, 1776	Thomas Paine publishes *Common Sense.*
March 17, 1776	British forced out of Boston by Patriot army.
July 4, 1776	Declaration of Independence adopted.
August 27, 1776	Battle of Long Island.
November 16, 1776	Fort Washington in Manhattan falls to the British.
December 25, 1776	Washington's army crosses the Delaware River.
September 26, 1777	British capture Philadelphia.
October 17, 1777	British army surrenders at Saratoga.
Winter of 1777-1778	American troops endure winter at Valley Forge.
February 1778	France signs treaty to help the Americans.
June 28, 1778	Battle of Monmouth, N.J.
1779-1780	British concentrate on winning in the southern colonies.
May 12, 1780	Charleston falls to the British.
January 17, 1781	Battle of Cowpens.
October 19, 1781	British surrender at Yorktown.
September 3, 1783	Treaty of Paris signed formally ending the war.
1787	Constitution of the United States written.
1789	Constitution ratified by the states.

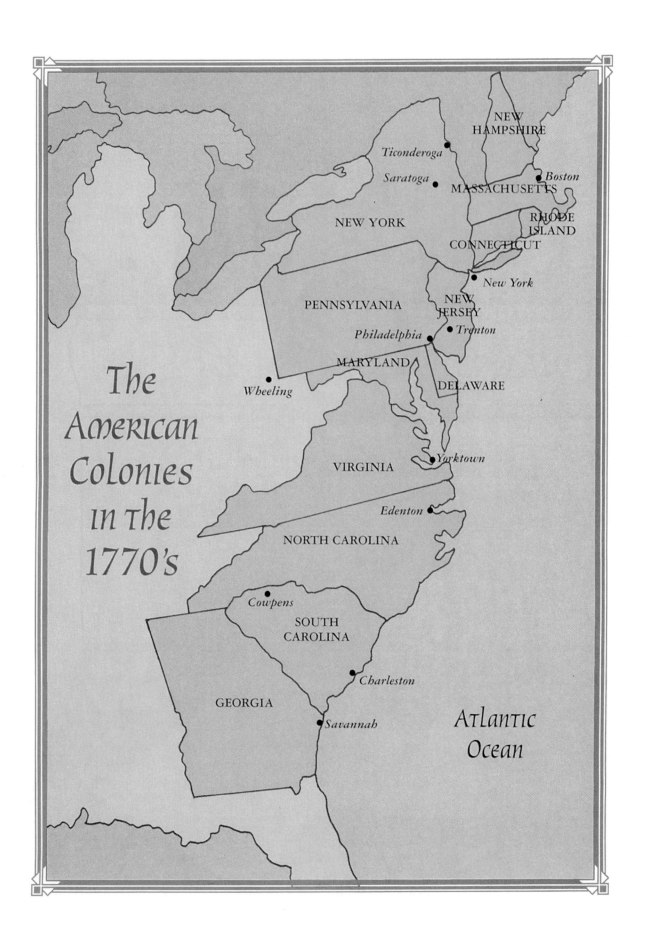

The
American
Colonies
in the
1770's

NEW
HAMPSHIRE

Ticonderoga

Saratoga

MASSACHUSETTS

Boston

NEW YORK

RHODE
ISLAND

CONNECTICUT

New York

PENNSYLVANIA

NEW
JERSEY

Philadelphia

Trenton

MARYLAND

DELAWARE

Wheeling

VIRGINIA

Yorktown

Edenton

NORTH CAROLINA

Cowpens

SOUTH
CAROLINA

Charleston

GEORGIA

Savannah

Atlantic
Ocean

7

Abigail Adams was a lover of liberty and a great writer of letters.

Abigail Adams was the wife of John Adams, the second president of the United States. Women in the 1770's were not supposed to be concerned about politics. Abigail Adams talked and wrote about politics with insight. She was one of the earliest supporters of independence for the Colonies. Her ideas influenced the founding fathers.

Abigail Adams
Champion for Equal Rights for Women

THE LIGHT SUMMER WIND ruffled her writing paper as Abigail Adams picked up her quill pen and wrote, "My dearest friend..." So began the many letters Abigail wrote to her husband, John Adams, a lawyer who became America's second president. Spanning 50 years, their letters paint a vivid picture of one of the most successful marriages in American history.

Abigail Smith was fourteen when she first met John Adams. Though it wasn't love at first sight, John was impressed with Abigail's mind. Often ill as a child, Abigail had educated herself in her father's library. Reading Shakespeare, Milton, Pope and other classics, she taught herself French and tried to learn Latin. Her parents encouraged all this learning even though it was unusual for a young woman of her day. She and John began exchanging love letters and after several years of courtship they married on Oct. 25, 1764.

For more than ten years of their married life, Abigail stayed at their farm in Massachusetts while John lived in Philadelphia serving in the Continental Congress and helping direct the American Revolutionary War. She was proud of how she managed their farm during the war. She wrote her friend Mercy

Warren, "I hope in time to have the Reputation of being as good a Farmeress as my partner has of being a good Statesman." John Adams was proud of his wife. He was also relieved his family of five children was well-maintained throughout the difficult war.

Few women were involved in politics in the 1700's. Abigail, though, was a trusted and shrewd advisor to her politician husband. She helped to shape his ideas, just as he helped to shape the country's ideas about freedom. Her influence with him was so great that some rival politicians eventually nick-named Abigail "Mrs. President." Two centuries later, the same term is still used for strong-minded first ladies.

Abigail supported the earliest efforts to gain freedom from England. Although creating a revolution was a daring idea, Abigail encouraged John to support it. Other leaders embraced this idea and it grew.

Abigail had another radical idea which was far ahead of her time. This idea was that women should have equality. She wrote to John at the Continental Congress:

> I long to hear that you have declared an independency... In the new Code of Laws which I suppose it will be necessary for you to make, I desire you would remember the ladies, and be more generous and favorable to them than your ancestors. Do not put such unlimited power into the hands of the husbands. Remember all men would be tyrants if they could. If particular care and attention is not paid to the ladies we are determined to foment a rebellion, and will not hold ourselves bound by any laws in which we have no voice or representation.

During the American Revolutionary War, her many letters were lively and full of the details of everyday life. She wrote to her husband, her friends and many who were involved in the revolution. She wrote of how her small town of Braintree was overrun with refugees from Boston, of the urgent need the women of her community had for sewing pins, and of the saltpeter women were making in their homes to be used in gunpowder for the Patriot army.

In her letters Abigail spoke her mind as well. On the issue of slavery she wrote, "As for the passion for liberty among the men from Virginia, how strong can it be since they have been accustomed to deprive their fellow creatures of theirs?"

Letters in Colonial Times

Letters in the 1700's were written on paper, folded, and sealed with wax without envelopes. Paper was too expensive to use for envelopes. Addresses were simple – often just the name of a town without a street address. In colonial days, the person receiving a letter paid the postage.

In another letter to John, weeks before he was inaugurated as President, she wrote that a neighbor was upset with her because she had sent a young black servant to evening school:

> The boy is a freeman as much as any of the young men. And merely because his face is black is he to be denied instruction? How is he to be qualified to procure a livelihood? I have not thought it any disgrace to myself to take him into my parlour and teach him both to read and write.

Lover of liberty and great writer of letters, Abigail did all she could to guide her young country toward freedom. She fought for freedom from England, freedom from slavery, and freedom from the inequality women suffered in her lifetime. Abigail would be proud to see how these freedoms have developed in the country she helped to found.

By early winter of 1776, General Washington's army had lost a series of battles to the British. At the end of August, the Patriot army was driven off Long Island. In October, they retreated from New York City. In November, Fort Washington and Fort Lee along the Hudson River were captured. It looked to some as if the British, the world's super power at the time, was too much for the ragtag Patriot army.

Hannah Arnett

The Patriot Wife Who Would Not Be Quiet

HANNAH FLUNG THE NEWSPAPER down on the dining table. "Ever since the Patriots declared independence from the king, things have been going badly," she thought.

From her house in Elizabethtown, New Jersey, Hannah could see by the winter of 1776 that the Patriots were losing the American Revolutionary War. That summer General Washington had moved his army to New York City to protect the city from the British. The British had more boats, more soldiers and better muskets. They drove General Washington out of New York City, across the Hudson River and into New Jersey.

Now that they had New York City, the British wanted to end the fighting as soon as possible. When Patriot leaders refused to surrender the British generals appealed directly to the American people. They issued a proclamation promising to pardon all Patriots who signed a Declaration of Allegiance to Great Britain.

There was a meeting to discuss the British offer at Hannah's house. Hannah, the Patriot wife, was not invited to the meeting so she sat for hours in the kitchen listening to the men talk about Washington's weak, half-starved army. "You have to admit Washington's army cannot hold out much longer," she heard one man saying.

"I agree," said another. "I have to think about my future and what is best for my family."

Finally Hannah put her cross-stitching down. She decided it was time to speak. She walked into the parlor and looking straight at them she took a deep breath and said, "Have you made your decision, gentlemen? I stand before you to know: have you chosen the part of men or traitors? If America should win in the conflict after you have thrown yourself on British clemency, where will you be then? God is on our side, and every volley of our muskets is an echo of his voice. We are poor, weak, and few, but God is fighting for

"Have you made your decision, gentlemen?"

us; we entered into this struggle with pure hearts and prayerful lips; we had counted the cost and were willing to pay the price. And now, because for a time the day is going against us, you would give up and sneak back to kiss the feet that have trampled upon us. You call yourselves men? Oh, shame upon you, cowards!" She went on, even threatening to leave her husband if these Patriots took the British offer.

When she finished there was silence in the room for a few moments. One of the men spoke, "I believe Mrs. Arnett has brought up a good point. Maybe we are acting too hasty and are basing our decision on what we think in our heads but not in our hearts." The man continued, "Gentlemen, I, for one, will not sign the proclamation. I will remain a Patriot."

Her husband stood up and walked over beside Hannah. "Gentlemen, I also agree," he said putting his arm around her. "My wife has shown me that my heart is with the Patriots' cause and I too will remain a Patriot." By the end of the evening all those who had gathered at Hannah's house agreed not to sign the proclamation. Hannah went to bed that night proud of herself for standing up for the fight for freedom and the new country she was so eager to live in.

Colonial Newspapers

In 1776, there were dozens of newspapers throughout the colonies. Most were only four pages long and came out weekly. Newspapers were very important in helping spread ideas before T.V. and radio. A tavern owner might subscribe to a newspaper and post it to draw patrons into his place. As the American Revolutionary War drew nearer, many newspapers grew bolder in their condemnation of the British. During the war some newspaper printers hid their presses to keep the British from seizing them.

Before the signing of the Declaration of Independence, men debated in local assemblies how to respond to British injustices. Women had no public outlet to express their convictions or to take a stand. Rebellion was considered men's business. Then the women of Edenton, North Carolina took a stand in 1774 that helped show women how they could oppose the British too.

Penelope Barker
Leader of the Edenton Tea Party

"I T'S NEVER BEEN DONE BY WOMEN, I tell you," Penelope Barker's husband said to her. She still held out the document she had asked him to read. "Never before have women protested against the British."

Penelope couldn't help sighing a little when she heard her husband's words. He must have heard her because he suddenly became more encouraging. He came over to where she was standing by the fire. "It's wonderful what you are doing." Penelope smiled at him. "But all I'm trying to say is the British may not take you seriously. You know how little they value a woman's opinion."

It was October 24, 1774 and the American Revolutionary War was still months off, but the spirit of independence was growing stronger in the American colonies. In the town of Edenton, North Carolina, a group of women were meeting to sign a declaration Penelope Barker had written. The declaration stated they would not drink tea from England or wear clothes made from British cloth.

Penelope Barker knew how little most men thought of a woman's opinion, but she knew in her heart the women of Edenton were going to do the right

thing. For years the British had been unfairly taxing the colonies. They taxed basic necessities like tea and cloth. They even taxed the space in colonist's homes. And most bothersome, the American colonists who were paying the taxes were not represented in the British Parliament.

Fifty-one women gathered in Elizabeth King's house to hear Penelope read her declaration. Penelope thought she was going to be nervous until she looked out into the crowd and saw how serious all the women's faces were. These were women she saw daily shopping and caring for their children.

"Maybe it has only been men who have protested the king up to now," Penelope began. "That only means we women have taken too long to let our voices be heard. We are signing our names to a document, not hiding ourselves behind costumes like the men in Boston did at their tea party. The British will know who we are."

When she finished reading her declaration Penelope asked if there were any questions. Mrs. Asbury raised her hand and said, "Yes, just one. May I be the first to sign it?" All the women laughed and stood up to sign the declaration.

The British did ridicule the women. Cartoons in the British newspapers showed the Edenton women signing the declaration and emptying their tea canisters. The British press called it the 'Edenton Tea Party' but the British could not ignore the fact women were now taking a stand. Soon women all over the colonies were boycotting British tea and cloth. The tax money the British wanted so much from the American colonies began to dwindle.

Penelope Barker's declaration gave every woman in America a way to rebel against the British. America's women then showed the British that they would not stand for taxation without representation.

Importance of Tea

In colonial times, tea drinking was a sign of sophistication and luxury. Tea was also considered healthier than plain water which was believed to sap the body's strength. Microscopic germs carrying diseases were still undiscovered.

The British insisted on taxing tea to prove they ruled the colonies. The British wanted the tea tax money to make colonial governors and judges dependent on England and not accountable to the local colonists.

◀ Mrs. Asbury raised her hand and said, "May I be the first to sign it?"

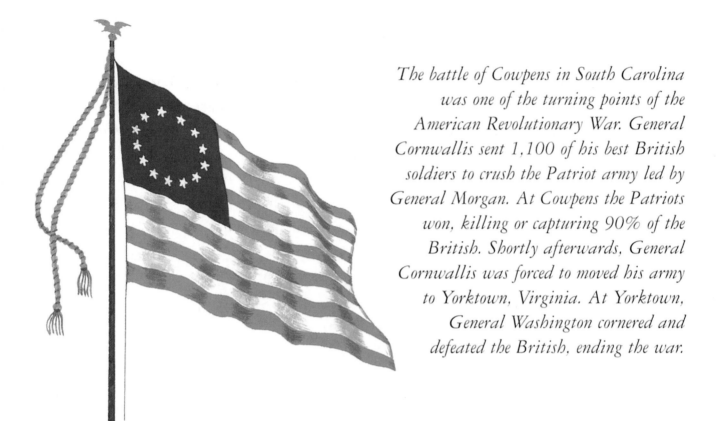

The battle of Cowpens in South Carolina was one of the turning points of the American Revolutionary War. General Cornwallis sent 1,100 of his best British soldiers to crush the Patriot army led by General Morgan. At Cowpens the Patriots won, killing or capturing 90% of the British. Shortly afterwards, General Cornwallis was forced to moved his army to Yorktown, Virginia. At Yorktown, General Washington cornered and defeated the British, ending the war.

Catherine Moore Barry

The Heroine of Cowpens

CATHERINE (KATE) BARRY KNEW the Patriots needed her help again. General Morgan with 600 men was fleeing from the British. General Morgan's sharpshooters had been a thorn in the British side throughout the American Revolutionary War. Now a British army nearly twice the size of Morgan's was out to get him for good.

Many times in the past Kate had been a scout and guide for the Patriots. She was as good on horseback as any man. And she knew the countryside and all the Indian trails for miles and miles. It was said that no group of Patriot soldiers had ever been caught by surprise when Kate was around. She had almost been caught by the British a number of times, but always managed to escape. Once, when Kate heard that the British soldiers were returning again, she had to tie her two-year-old daughter to the bed-post because there was no babysitter while she rode off to warn her husband and his men.

The Patriots in her area fought in small bands using hit-and-run tactics. Kate knew each group and where their hideouts were. She also helped them

Kate escaped the British many times.

by concealing food in the hollow trunks of trees so that they would always have something to eat, even on the run. General Morgan now needed more soldiers. He had a plan to defeat the British who were chasing him, but he did not have enough men. The General got word to Kate Barry. Could she round up all the local bands of Patriots and convince them to join in the fight with him? Kate knew she could. She knew how to find all the local Patriots. The Patriots knew they could trust Kate.

In less than two weeks General Morgan's army swelled to 1,600 men. The Patriots then allowed the British to catch them at Cowpens on January 17, 1781. General Morgan's plan worked so well that only twelve Patriot soldiers were killed while the British army was destroyed. Without all the reinforcements, General Morgan's army would have been the one destroyed. Kate Barry was acclaimed far and wide as the heroine of Cowpens.

In 1780 the British nearly controlled South Carolina. Many Patriots had fled or taken oaths not to fight against the king. Marauding bands of British loyalists terrorized the few remaining Patriots. One turning point that rallied Patriot morale in South Carolina took place near Martha Bratton's home. After that battle more Patriots returned to join the local militias. The reinforcements led to a series of Patriot victories.

Martha Bratton
A Brave and Compassionate Patriot Woman

BY THE SUMMER OF 1780 it seemed to Martha Bratton the American Revolutionary War would never end. In Charleston, South Carolina many patriots started giving up hope that they might win the war, especially after the city surrendered to the British. Over 5,000 men were taken prisoner and most of the Patriot supplies for the state were captured.

British troops roaming the South Carolina countryside met little resistance in the following months. Americans were offered the choice of accepting British protection or imprisonment. An English general boasted that in the southern colonies the American Revolutionary War had ended.

Gunpowder, like many other items, was scarce during this time. Martha Bratton, and her husband had been entrusted by the American governor of South Carolina to hold a supply of the precious powder. When her husband was away fighting for the Patriots, Martha was responsible for the gunpowder.

Martha lit the trail of gunpowder ▶

The British found out where it was hidden and decided to steal it. Martha heard of their plan. "They'll wish they had never come here," she smiled as she walked over to the kegs of gunpowder.

Martha had a plan of her own. "I know where the British are coming from. I'll lay a trail of gunpowder going the other way. There will be a big surprise waiting for them Redcoats." Martha decided that just when the soldiers got near the supplies she would light the trail of gunpowder and blow up all the ammunition. "It's the last thing they'll be expecting," she thought.

After she finished laying her trail Martha hid in the woods. As the British approached, she raced to where the gunpowder trail lay and lit a match to it. In less than a minute she heard a huge explosion and men screaming.

Running away from the explosion, Martha was caught by the British. The British commander demanded to know who had set the gunpowder on fire. Martha looked him straight in the face and answered, "It was I who did it. Let the consequence be what it will. I glory in having prevented the mischief contemplated by the cruel enemies of my country." Unexpectedly, the British let Martha go free as they marched off.

When the British authorities heard of the gunpowder incident and that it was hidden at the Bratton's house they came looking for Martha's husband. He was not there and Martha refused

Gunpowder

Gunpowder is a mixture of potassium nitrate (which the colonists called saltpeter), charcoal and sulphur. Used to fire guns and cannons, the British made it illegal for colonists to produce or import gunpowder at the beginning of the American Revolutionary War. The Patriots set up their own manufacturing sites but were often low on gunpowder.

to tell the British where her husband had gone. The head British officer became furious with Martha. Picking up a reaping hook he threatened to slash her throat. Martha stood in front of her children, refusing to give up any information. The British lieutenant begged the senior officer to let Martha go. With a nasty glance at his subordinate, the officer finally agreed.

He then ordered Martha to make dinner for all the British soldiers. After dinner the English troops left Martha's house, retiring to another farm a half-mile away.

Later that night, Martha's husband came home. Martha told him where the British were camped. Although the Patriot band was outnumbered they launched a surprise attack. Some British soldiers were killed including the senior officer. Others were wounded and some taken prisoner. A few managed to escape.

The lieutenant who had pleaded for Martha's life was now the leader of the British troops. When he was captured many Patriots wanted to hang him as an example. The officer asked for one last favor, and that was to be brought before Martha Bratton. Martha instantly recognized him as the officer who had saved her life. Despite all the hardships and dangers the British had put Martha and her family through, she pleaded with the Patriots to spare this honorable and decent man. Because of Martha's speech, he was not hanged.

Martha realized how cruel people were becoming from the fighting of the American Revolutionary War. She wanted to remind everyone that freedom required tolerance and love even for your enemies. So she turned her house into a hospital and nursed both British and American soldiers.

Many American prisoners-of-war during the American Revolutionary War were kept on prison ships in New York Harbor. Conditions there were horrible. Prisoners had little clothing, no heat, and dirty water to drink. Disease was rampant. Over 7,000 Patriot soldiers died in captivity on the prison ships.

Elizabeth Burgin

Organizer of the Great Prisoner Escape

ELIZABETH BURGIN HAD SEEN NEW YORK CITY become a cold, unhappy place for the Patriots during the American Revolutionary War. The British were holding captured American soldiers in the harbor. Prisoners were crowded onto ships and given little food or water. The senior British officer in charge treated the prisoners very badly. He starved, hanged or poisoned prisoners who displeased him. Elizabeth Burgin was determined to help these Patriot prisoners.

Visiting the prisoners as often as she could, Elizabeth brought them food. Elizabeth dreaded the trips to the prison ships. It hurt her so much to see the prisoners' faces. Their eyes had lost life and hope. The prisoners were covered in dirt and most of them didn't even look human to her. They looked like scared animals. "That's about all they are," Elizabeth thought as she filled a soup bowl for one of them and handed him the hot broth. This could be his last meal, she thought bitterly. She wished she could fight the ruthlessness of the British.

Elizabeth smiled at the prisoner but he could only manage a blank stare back at her. All the way back to her house, she thought of the Patriot soldiers trapped on the ships. She thought to herself, "If only there was some way I could just climb into that ship and free them all." Pulling her cloak around herself tighter, she walked down the cobblestone street to her home.

When she arrived home she was surprised to see a Patriot officer standing by her door. "What could he possibly want?" she wondered.

"Good evening Mrs. Burgin," the officer said tipping his hat to her. "I was wondering if I could speak to you for a few minutes."

"Yes, come in. I've just gotten back from the prison ship," she said, opening the door.

"That's exactly what I want to talk to you about," he replied. Elizabeth listened intently as the officer spoke.

"We have a plan to help prisoners escape from the ships," he said. "And we need your help."

"My help!" Elizabeth answered with surprise. "What can I possibly do to help them escape?"

"You and the other ladies are the only ones the British will let near the prisoners. We need you at least to get them word of our

Prison Ships

The British converted old navy ships into floating prisons during the American Revolutionary War. Packed with as many as 1,100 prisoners on board, ventilation was poor while smallpox and yellow fever spread easily. Some British officers were very cruel to the prisoners, while others tried to treat them decently.

plans. We also need help smuggling them out." Elizabeth's wish had come true. She was going to be able to help the prisoners escape. She couldn't stop thinking about the haunting eyes of that prisoner who had stared at her as she fed him soup.

Over the next weeks Elizabeth assisted in the escape of over 200 prisoners. George Washington wrote to the Continental Congress about her valiant work:

Regarding Elizabeth Burgin, recently an inhabitant of New York. From the testimony of our own (escaped) officers... it would appear that she has been indefatigable for the relief of the prisoners, and for the facilitation of their escape. For this conduct she incurred the suspicion of the British, and was forced to make her escape under disturbing circumstances.

General Washington knew that Elizabeth Burgin was in danger. The British had offered 200 pounds for her capture, an amount equal to twenty years' pay for a British soldier. He knew she had to escape from New York.

One night Elizabeth secretly boarded a whaleboat to make her escape. She was almost captured on her flight. Two British boats chased the whaleboat half-way to New England before they gave up.

Elizabeth was determined to help the patriot prisoners.

After her escape, Elizabeth was left without anything but her children. She wrote to General George Washington, pleading with him to help, since the British had taken all her possessions.

"I am now, sir, very destitute, without money or clothes or friends to go to. God knows how I shall live through the cold winter that is coming. Helping our poor prisoners has brought me to this, but I don't regret it."

In 1781, Congress awarded Elizabeth a pension for her services to Patriot soldiers during the American Revolutionary War. She was thankful for the money and even more thankful for the chance to help her fellow Patriots when they needed her.

Fort Washington was built near New York City as part of the Patriot defense system. In November 1776, the British seized the fort in one of the worse Patriot defeats of the American Revolutionary War.

Margaret Corbin

Captain Molly

THE PAIN SHOT THROUGH MARGARET CORBIN'S ARM. As she opened her eyes in agony, she saw her husband lying dead beside her. She tried to reach over to the cannon they had been manning together. Then everything started spinning around. As she tried to take a deep breath, she collapsed beside her husband.

When Margaret Corbin was five she lost her parents in an Indian raid. Margaret then lived with her uncle until she married John Corbin in 1772. When John signed up with the Continental Army, Margaret went with him. "I don't want you leaving me alone," she said.

Margaret became a camp follower as did many women during the American Revolutionary War. These women traveled with the Patriot army. They lived in the camp with their husbands or fathers while cooking, washing clothes, and serving as nurses. The camp followers provided all these valuable services for the Patriot army without pay.

◀ Margaret began work on loading the cannon.

When Margaret and her husband joined the Patriot army, they were stationed at Fort Washington in New York City. The British army had already captured most of New York City. Everyone knew Fort Washington would be their next target.

John begged Margaret to go home. They argued in voices that could barely be heard over the still night air. "I want you out of here by day break," he said to her. "I'm the soldier, Margaret. Go to our home."

"You may be the soldier, John Corbin, but I am you're wife and my place is by your side. If the battle is going to be bad, how can I leave now when I'm most needed?" Margaret was determined to stay.

Camp Followers

Many wives, mothers and daughters of Patriot soldiers followed their husbands, sons and fathers when they entered the army. Some women followed their men into the army to help the Patriot cause and some went because they could not support themselves alone. Called "camp followers," these women helped the Patriot army with cooking, washing, mending, and nursing. They also required food, tents, and transportation which sometimes strained the army's resources.

During the battle, John served as a matross for a cannon. He worked beside the gunner, loading and sponging the cannon. When the battle started, John and the gunner fired the cannon rapidly. They could barely hear each other over all the cannon fire and screams surrounding them.

Then the gunner was killed. As John looked down at the gunner, he felt a hand on his shoulder. Turning around, he saw Margaret standing behind him. She motioned for him to take over as the gunner. She began work as the matross.

The British army kept coming up the rugged hillside toward the Patriot soldiers. As the British came closer, the sounds of the battle grew deafening. Margaret's ears were ringing from all the noise. As she was reaching around for her sponge, she heard a blast. It killed her husband. Shocked, Margaret had knelt down to touch his face when she was hit too.

As Margaret and John lay beside each other, the British troops took over Fort Washington and captured the Patriot soldiers. Margaret Corbin was left for dead. That afternoon, a doctor who had been sent to recover the wounded walked past her. As he turned away, he saw Margaret's hand move towards him. He realized the badly wounded person before him was a woman. Margaret had severe chest and jaw wounds, and her left arm was nearly torn from her body. The doctor gathered her up and put her on a wagon that would take her to a hospital in Philadelphia.

Margaret Corbin was permanently disabled from her wounds, with her face and arm badly scarred. In July 1777, her heroism was recognized by Congress. They made her a part of the Invalid Regiment, soldiers who had been disabled fighting for freedom. She became known as "Captain Molly." After the American Revolutionary War, she was the first woman to receive a lifetime pension for the wounds she suffered in battle.

In December of 1777, British troops were occupying Philadelphia. General Washington's army was camped at Whitemarsh, 13 miles away. The Patriots harassed the larger British army from Whitemarsh. On the night of December 4, the British planned to march 12,000 troops out of Philadelphia for a surprise attack on the Patriot position.

Lydia Darragh

Quaker Woman of Conscience

FROST NEARLY COVERED THE OUTSIDE of the window as Lydia Darragh watched the British headquarters across the street from her house. Winter was going to be even bleaker this year with the British occupying Philadelphia, she thought. Lydia and her husband were members of the Society of Friends, also known as Quakers. The British knew their religion prohibited them from becoming involved in the war. The British found this convenient and often used the Darraghs' house to hold meetings.

One day an officer informed Lydia that her family needed to be in bed early that night. The British staff was going to hold an important meeting in her house. "This is odd," Lydia thought to herself as she watched the soldier walk back across the street. "They've never asked us to stay in bed during their meetings."

"I need to talk to you in private."

She told her family about the meeting over dinner. "He told me they were going to hold a meeting at our house tonight and they want us all in bed by eight."

"Another meeting," her husband said. "This war sure does call for a lot of meetings. I can't help but think about all those young boys dying on both sides while these all-important meetings are going on."

Lydia shook her head in agreement, but thought, "He's not the least bit suspicious about us all having to be in bed." During the prayer she asked God for guidance that night when the British came.

At eight o' clock the officers came and Lydia showed them to their room. She then went to her bedroom, but she didn't sleep. She tip-toed down the hall to the meeting room. She strained to hear what the officers were saying.

Their voices were muffled, but she heard one of them clearly. "The British troops are to leave Philadephia on the night of the fourth and attack General Washington's camp at Whitemarsh."

Lydia walked quietly back to her room. When the officer knocked on the door to let her know they were leaving, Lydia got up slowly so he would think she had been asleep.

Beds

Many colonial beds were four-posters. Each of the four corners had a tall post upon which the bed frame was built. On top of the posts was a canopy called a tester. Curtains hanging down added extra warmth in winter. There were no bed springs; instead ropes tied across the frame supported the mattress. People who could afford it would have feather mattresses. Others had mattresses stuffed with woolen rags or straw. Families slept in the same room and sometimes in the same bed for warmth.

All night she lay awake praying about what she should do. If she told no one, then many young American Patriots would die. By morning she had her answer.

"I can't tell my husband," she thought, putting her coat on. "It's much too dangerous to share this information with anyone."

Lydia pretended she had to go to the mill outside of town to buy flour. When she got to there, she left her sack at the mill to be filled. Lydia started walking towards the American camp at Whitemarsh. On the way she met a Patriot officer. "I need to talk to you in private," she said. Lydia told him of the attack that was going to take place.

"Please, you must not tell anyone that I have told you," she pleaded to him. "I do not want my family in danger." The officer promised and Lydia headed towards home relieved.

She took a few steps and stopped short. "I have to be sure this message gets through! It is too important to chance!" Lydia turned and headed back again towards the American camp at Whitemarsh. Walking a few miles more, she came upon another Patriot officer, someone she knew. Giving him the same message about the attack, Lydia felt confident the word would get back to General Washington.

On the night of the fourth, she heard the British troops leave town heading towards Whitemarsh. Her heart started racing as the sound of the soldiers marching faded in the distance. After the British returned, without the victory they expected, Lydia was summoned by the British general. He asked her if anyone in her house had been awake during their meeting. "Sir," she said, "I made sure my whole family was asleep."

"Somehow the Patriots found out about us," he said, still eyeing her. "They were ready for us."

When Lydia finally walked out the door, her hands were sweating and her heart was beating fast. Looking up to the sky she said, "Thank you, God, for giving me strength." Lydia knew in her heart she had done the right thing for her religion and her country.

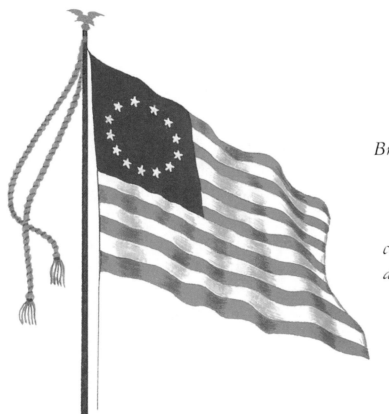

In summer of 1781, Patriot General Nathaniel Greene had retreated to the Broad River in South Carolina. The British greatly outnumbered his army. He desperately needed reinforcements from Patriot General Thomas Sumter who was camped by the Wateree River. The countryside was full of British loyalists and it was a dangerous journey for any courier to get the message through.

Emily Geiger
The Quick-Thinking Messenger

GENERAL GREENE'S PATRIOT ARMY WAS IN TROUBLE. The general needed a messenger to take a letter to General Sumter and his army 100 miles away. If he didn't get help the British might corner his army and defeat it. General Greene asked the local farmers for a volunteer who knew the countryside. A girl of sixteen came forward.

"My name's Emily Geiger. I know the countryside and I think I can get through for you." Even though he had asked for a man to carry this message, the situation was desperate and General Greene agreed to send Emily.

"This could be dangerous. If they catch you with a message, you might be killed. The British punish spies with hanging," he warned her.

"Then I'll memorize the message," said Emily.

"Ah, but then General Sumter may not believe you. He knows my handwriting," the general replied.

"You could do both. Write out the message. If I have to destroy it, I'll still know what to tell him," Emily told him. General Greene decided to do both. Once Emily had memorized the message she rode off. She knew how important her mission was. She traveled fast and stayed out of sight. The first day and first night the British did not spot her.

On the second day, the British caught her. "Where was she going? What was she doing?" they asked. They led her to a farm house and put her in a bedroom.

"Send for a woman to search her," the British officer said as he locked the door of the bedroom. The men hadn't looked inside Emily's clothes where she had the letter hidden. The room offered no escape. Emily had to think quickly. In a few minutes a woman showed up to search Emily. She ordered Emily to undress. Every inch of clothing was searched and turned inside out. No message was found. The woman looked around the room and saw nothing suspicious. She led Emily out of the bedroom. The British soldiers let Emily go.

Emily knew the British soldiers were still watching her. She didn't head directly for General Sumter's camp. Instead she headed away from the Patriot army and then circled around to be safe. It took her an extra day to reach Sumter's army. She told the first Patriot soldier she met to take her to General Sumter. "I have an important message for you, General," she said when she arrived at his headquarters.

"Well, let me read it," he demanded.

"You can't" said Emily. She recited to him the message she had memorized. So that the general would believe her, she described her trip to reach him.

"Send for a woman to search her," said the British officer.

"I have just one question, "said General Sumter. "When you were alone in the room, what did you do with the letter?"

"I ate it!" replied Emily. "No other meal did so much to keep me alive and healthy."

General Sumter gave orders for his army to march and join up with General Greene. When the British army discovered Patriot reinforcements were coming, they retreated. Emily Geiger's bravery and quick thinking saved the day for General Greene's Patriot army.

Travel in the 1770's

Travel was always difficult and sometimes dangerous. Roads were not paved. Outside of towns, roads tended to be narrow, winding and unmarked. Many rivers and streams did not have bridges. If there was a ferry, travelers might have to pay a ferryman to take them across a river.

The fighting in Georgia during the American Revolutionary War was fierce. It was called the "war of extermination." Many Patriot wives and children from the countryside moved to Tennessee for safety. One woman, Nancy Hart, stayed. Her home became an outpost for Patriot scouts and soldiers.

Nancy Hart

The War Woman of Broad River

"I DON'T HAVE MUCH USE FOR THE KING OR HIS MEN," said Nancy Hart as she eyed the five British soldiers who were seated around her table. "They have taken from my family and friends and left me with nothing. I have no use for them." Nancy Hart, who lived in Georgia along the Broad River, was known for her strength and outspokenness. When most woman and children had been removed from the area because of British attacks, she had remained to fight for her home.

British soldiers had heard that Nancy once helped a rebel escape from them. They had come to ask Nancy if the story was true.

"Sure, the story is true," she said proudly. "And if you want I'll tell you about it now. It was a day much like today, kind of quiet and not much going on. I heard this horse galloping up the road and looked out my window here to see a young Patriot riding towards my house. I knew what was wrong the minute I saw him. A bunch of British soldiers had to be chasing him. I let the bars down to my house and told that young fellow to ride right through here and out the back door and hide in the swamp. And that is just what he

Nancy aimed a musket at the British.

did. Well, it wasn't much later when some British soldiers came up and asked if I had seen anyone riding by. I pretended I was a sick old woman, so they wouldn't recognize me and I told them I had seen a man ride up into the woods. They took off into the woods after him," she said, laughing. Looking around the room she could tell her story had not pleased her visitors.

"Fix us something to eat," the soldiers demanded.

"I never feed traitors or king's men if I can help it. The scamps have run off with all my pigs and poultry, except for that one turkey in the yard. I haven't anything to feed you," she told them gruffly.

"Now you do," a soldier said as he shot her turkey.

Nancy reluctantly started to prepare the turkey and began listening to the conversation of the soldiers. They started bragging about how they had murdered Colonel Dooley that morning. Colonel Dooley was a Patriot and Nancy's friend.

Nancy told her daughter to go sound the conch shell. The shell signaled the neighbors that there were British soldiers about. Then she began to joke and laugh with the British soldiers. By the time Nancy had dinner ready, they were drinking from a jug of rum. As Nancy served them dinner, she had her daughter go and get some drinking water from the well. "Also," Nancy said, "sound the conch shell again to tell our Patriot friends to come."

While the British soldiers were eating, Nancy pulled some boards off the house and slid two of the soldiers' muskets out through the hole. One of the soldiers saw her and stood up. As soon as he did, Nancy aimed a musket towards him and shouted, "I'll shoot the first one of you that moves." One of the soldiers moved toward her. Nancy shot him dead and then quickly snatched up another of the British muskets.

Her daughter came back and told Nancy help was on the way. When the soldiers heard this, they decided to charge at Nancy as a group. Nancy shot and killed another soldier. Her daughter quickly handed her another gun. She aimed it at the remaining men and they stayed back. When her neighbors arrived, they wanted to shoot the remaining British soldiers, but Nancy told them the news of Colonel Dooley's murder. "Shooting's too good for them. Let's hang them," she said, and so they did.

Nancy's reputation of risking herself for the Patriot cause was widely known. When the Patriots needed information about what the British were planning to do in Augusta, Georgia, she dressed up as a man. She went into the British camp acting crazy. Nancy kept up her disguise for several days, uncovered the needed information, and returned with it to the Patriots.

Nancy's aggressive nature was common knowledge. In the wilds of Georgia it brought her honor. The Liberty Boys (her name for American Patriots) called her "Aunt" Nancy Hart. The Indians named a nearby stream 'War Woman Creek' after her. The state of Georgia did even better. They honored Nancy Hart by naming a county after her and placing her portrait in the state capital rotunda.

In the spring of 1777, the British were hoping to cut short the American Revolutionary War. British troops from New York set out to destroy Patriot supply centers in Connecticut and upstate New York. Sybil Ludington was sixteen when she rode over twenty-five miles to warn the local miltia the British were coming. She rode more than twice as far as Paul Revere's famous ride.

Sybil Ludington
The Female Paul Revere

O N A BEAUTIFUL APRIL NIGHT IN 1777, Sybil Ludington wished on a star that the American Revolutionary War would soon be over. As made her wish that night, Sybil had no idea that twenty-five miles away from her home the British were burning the town of Danbury, Connecticut. Two thousand British soldiers had descended on the town to destroy it's Patriot supply center. After sacking Danbury, the British were headed to her town of Fredricksburg, New York.

Sybil's father, Colonel Ludington, was in charge of the area's volunteer militia. He had no idea what a long night was in front of him and his daughter. Sybil had just blown out the candles in the upstairs bedrooms when she heard a horse come racing down the street. Then there was a loud pounding at their front door. Curious, she raced down the steps and reached the door at the same time as her father.

"Who could it be this late?" she asked him as he unbolted the door. A very young and exhausted American soldier who looked as if he hadn't slept in

"The British are heading this way," cried out Sybil. ▶

days was on the doorstep. His hat was pushed to one side and his pants were torn around the legs. "What is it, son?" said Colonel Ludington as he helped the young man into the house. The soldier began to tell them about the burning of Danbury and how the British troops were heading towards Fredericksburg.

"Your men must be alerted," he said. "My horse and I are too tired to go on. Is there anyone who could go?"

"I'd go myself," said Sybil's father, "but I need to be here when the men arrive."

Without even thinking, Sybil spoke up. "I'll go and alert the men," she said with confidence. Before her mother or father could object, she went on. "You know I can ride better than any man in town and my horse Star is as swift as the wind."

"You must hurry," warned the soldier. "The British are on their way right now." Sybil ran out the door with her father close behind. On the way to the barn she grabbed a large stick so she could bang on people's doors as she rode through the towns. Her father helped her get on her horse and said, "You be careful, Sybil. This could end up being a very dangerous night. Come back as soon as you are through."

The roads she and Star had to travel were little more than well-worn paths from one village to the next. As she reached towns with names of Kent Cliffs, Mahopac and Farmers Mills, she knocked on each door to rouse the militia. "Meet at Colonel Ludington's house immediately," she yelled through the streets. "The British have burned Danbury and they are heading this way." Sybil was aware of the danger in her ride through the countryside. British spies, wild animals, or Indians could be behind every turn.

When she arrived back at her house, the Patriot minutemen were already gathering. Soon her father led them to intercept the British at Ridgefield. There the Patriots drove the British back to their ships on Long Island Sound. The next day the British forces sailed away.

When Sybil's father came into her room the next morning, he said, "You were as brave as any man who fought with me last night." For her bravery and because her call to arms helped drive the British away, Sybil Ludington became known as the female Paul Revere.

Grace and Rachel Martin lived in South Carolina with their mother-in-law during the American Revolutionary War. Both their husbands along with five other men from the Martin family fought for the Patriots. By 1780, the British controlled most of the southern colonies. Then General Nathaniel Greene led a hit-and-run campaign against the British. In less than one year the British were retreating from most of their positions in the southern colonies.

Grace and Rachel Martin

Interceptors of the Courier

"GRACE, MEET ME BY THE WELL," said Rachel as they passed on the steps of their mother-in-law's house one spring morning. "I'll be there in about ten minutes." Grace had no idea what her sister-in-law wanted, but she could tell by the look on Rachel's face that it must be something important. She finished making her bed and then walked out the back door of the house to the well. Rachel was holding some daffodils that she had picked along the way. Her hair was blowing in the breeze. She looked so innocent standing there! "Whatever could she be up to?" thought Grace as she walked closer.

"Come here," said Rachel, pulling Grace near to her.

"What I am about to tell you is very important and you must not say a word to another soul." As Grace nodded, Rachel continued. "I have found out that tonight a British courier is coming by our road. He is going to be carrying important documents and we must stop him somehow."

Grace looked at her sister-in-law with surprise. "You want us to stop a British courier tonight?" she asked. "And just how do you plan to do that?"

Marriage

In the 1700's most all men and women got married. Bachelors and spinsters were looked down upon. Divorce was rare. People were encouraged to marry young and start large families. Children spent little time in school and helped with farmwork and household chores.

Since there was no Social Security, people depended on their children and grandchildren to support them when they were too old to work. Thus, having many children was like having insurance. Women could own property they inherited. But as soon as they married, their husbands took control of the property.

"We'll dress up in our husbands' clothes and take their pistols. We'll just scare them and they'll never know we are women."

"Wait a minute," said Grace, getting more nervous. "You said there was a British courier. What is this about 'them'?"

"I forgot to tell you," Rachel said looking down at the flowers. "There are going to be two British officers guarding him."

Grace thought about what Rachel had told her for a few minutes. Just like everyone else, she was tired of how the British had treated the women and children who had been left behind while their husbands were out fighting the war. Just two months ago British soldiers had come to her mother-in-law's house and torn up all the feather beds looking for messages. She also thought about how her husband had been gone for such a long time fighting. Now this was her opportunity to do something to help.

"All right," she said, smiling at Rachel. "I'll do it."

They told their mother-in-law of their plan and she endorsed it. Their mother-in-law had seven sons who were all fighting as Patriots in the American Revolutionary War. "Now I don't have to tell you both to be careful," she warned her two daughters-in-law as she checked their pistols one more time. "Those British can be so tricky."

Grace and Rachel promised they would be careful. As evening fell they hid by the road where they meant to ambush the courier. As they sat in the grass

◄ "Hand over those documents and we'll let you go!"

the night seemed to get quieter and quieter. "The only thing I can hear is the grass blowing in the breeze," said Grace as she looked up at the stars in the sky. The women waited until they heard the sound of horses approaching. When the riders were almost on top of them, Grace and Rachel sprang up from the ground and leveled their pistols at the British.

"We know you carry important documents," said Rachel in a low voice. "Hand them over and we'll let you go unharmed." Looking at the two guns pointed at them, the surprised British soldiers quickly surrendered the papers. Grace grabbed them as Rachel kept a gun aimed at the men. Then the two women ran off into the woods with their prize. They wanted to get the papers as fast as possible to the Patriot Army. "We did it! We did it!" yelled Rachel as they raced through the woods.

Grace called back to her, "I know we did, but I have never been so scared in my whole life." The women passed the information safely to Patriot soldiers and headed home. When they arrived they were surprised to see their mother-in-law had guests. The guests were the British soldiers they had ambushed! The British had stopped at the house to ask if they could spend the night. Their mother-in-law had agreed to let them stay to avoid any suspicion.

Luckily Grace and Rachel had changed clothes out in the barn. Not once during the evening did the British couriers ever suspect that their hostesses, Grace and Rachel, were the men who had stolen their documents just down the road!

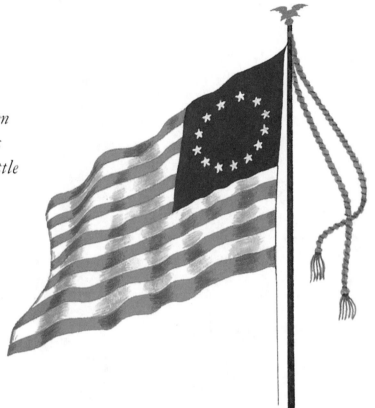

The battle of Monmouth was fought on June 28, 1778, near Trenton, New Jersey. It was the Patriot army's first open field battle with the British after months of training and drilling in European battle tactics. Facing the British on their own terms, the Americans claimed the victory.

Molly Hays McCauley
Molly Pitcher

O N ONE OF THE HOTTEST DAYS of the American Revolutionary War, the battle of Monmouth, New Jersey was fought. The Patriots had marched eighty miles in sweltering heat to fight the British. It was so hot a day that General Washington's horse collapsed.

Molly Hays McCauley struggled to keep the soldiers supplied with water during the battle. Going from one soldier to the next she waited as they gulped down the water. "You're coming back soon, aren't you?" they would ask as she started to walk off. Seeing her coming, soldiers called out, "Molly, bring a pitcher!" Then in the pitch of battle they shortened it to, "Molly! Pitcher!" In this way Molly Hays McCauley earned the nickname "Molly Pitcher."

While carrying water, Molly caught a glimpse of her husband, John, just as a British bullet hit his shoulder. She saw him tumble to the ground. Molly lifted her long dusty skirt and ran as fast as she could across the field to where he had been manning a cannon. She came to him and grabbed his arm where

Cannons

Cannons were large guns made of iron or brass. To load them, a soldier put in the gunpowder with a long ladle. Then one or two men shoved in a cannon ball (one big ball to put a hole in a wall or fort) or grapeshot (many smaller balls to break the enemy line). Using a ramrod, a soldier called the matross packed the contents tightly. Then the gunner touched a burning torch to a small hole in the rear of the cannon igniting the gunpowder.

he had been shot. "Don't worry, John, I'm here." She tore a piece off the bottom of her skirt and wrapped it tightly around his arm.

A Patriot soldier helping the wounded knelt beside her. "Mrs. McCauley," he said, taking her husband from her arms, "we'll take good care of him. You can come around to see him in a little while." Seeing that her husband was in good hands, Molly made a quick decision.

"I'll take over where he left off," Molly said. She went over to his cannon. She made sure it was aimed at the oncoming British. "I'll show the British there is plenty of fight left in us Patriots," she said, firing her first shot.

As the Patriot soldiers realized Molly had the skill to handle a cannon, the sight of her boosted their morale. The Patriot army cheered as Molly continued firing shot after shot. The Patriots fought with renewed enthusiasm. The British eventually retreated.

The next day General Washington asked Molly to come to his tent. "I wanted to thank you for all that you did yesterday," General Washington said to her. "You were a very brave woman. I am commissioning you as a sergeant in the Continental Army." This wasn't something that happened to women, only to men.

"Why thank you, sir," she said reaching out to shake his hand. "I am very honored that you think I am worthy of this."

◀ "I'll show the British there is plenty of fight left in us Patriots."

"More than worthy, Mrs. McCauley. I shall call you Sergeant Molly Pitcher, as the men do," General Washington said, smiling at her.

Molly and her husband both lived through the American Revolutionary War. After the war they returned to their home in Pennsylvania. She was awarded a military pension from the state of Pennsylvania in 1822. When she died, Molly Pitcher received a full military funeral.

Rebecca Motte's house stood above the Congaree River in South Carolina. The British were using it as a depot and as one of a group of strategic forts. In May of 1781, the Patriots had captured some of these forts in South Carolina. For the Patriots to drive the British from the South, they needed to take Rebecca's house back.

Rebecca Motte
The Patriot Who Burned Her Home

REBECCA RELUCTANTLY LOOKED BACK AT HER HOME as British soldiers led her away. They would be using her house as a base while they fought against the Patriots in the American Revolutionary War. "I'll be back," she thought to herself. "I'll get my house back no matter what it takes."

With the death of her husband early in the war, Rebecca had to care for her three daughters on her own. She had lived near Charleston most of her life. Now her home was high above the Congaree River northeast of Charleston. Due to its strong construction and easily defended position, it was called a fort, but to Rebecca it was home.

During the American Revlutionary War the Motte mansion had been a Patriot headquarters as well as a hospital. Rebecca was glad to lend her home to the Patriots. She had stayed to help the wounded soldiers at the hospital there.

In 1781, the British took over the Motte mansion. At first they permitted Rebecca and her children to stay in a part of the house. Then Patriot troops moved back into the area. The British decided that Rebecca might spy and tell their secrets to the Patriot army.

Of course Rebecca didn't want to leave her home and her possessions in the hands of the British. It made her mad to think that they were forcing her out. As she was walking down the hall escorted out by British soldiers, she noticed some fire arrows. Rebecca stopped to stuff the fire arrows into the bag she was

FIRE ARROWS

Fire arrows don't look very different from other arrows. A cloth soaked in pitch (a sticky paste that comes from pine trees) is tied to the end of the shaft and lit. When the arrow is shot, the pitch keeps burning. Once the arrow hits the target, the flaming pitch helps spread the fire.

carrying. She had no idea what she was going to do with them, but she didn't want the British to have them. "Right this way," said one of the soldiers as he grabbed her arm to lead her out.

"I know very well how to get out of my own home, thank you," she said staring him straight in the eye. "And you will be surprised at how fast I get back into my home." She left Fort Motte and moved in with the Patriots. When she arrived at the American camp, she was told the Patriot generals wanted to see her. They needed information about the British and their occupation of her home at Fort Motte. Rebecca told them that she felt the British were there to stay.

When the Patriots told her they wanted to drive the British out by burning her house down, Rebecca said, "If my house is going to be burned I have just the weapons for the job." Rebecca showed the Patriots her fire arrows.

When the Patriots attacked, they shot Rebecca's fire arrows onto the roof. Soon the top bedrooms caught on fire. The British became trapped in the burning mansion at Fort Motte. They had no choice but to surrender. Once the British left, Patriot troops rushed in to put out the fire. They put out the fire so quickly that only the top floor was burned. After the fire was extinguished, Rebecca served dinner to the Patriot officers in her smoke-stained dining room.

"Though I'm used to entertaining in a finer setting, this is one of happiest meals I have ever served," she told the Patriots as they raised their glasses to toast their victory.

◀ Rebecca watched as her house burned.

On September 15, 1776, General Washington's army was retreating from the British on Manhattan Island in New York City. The British navy had brought troops around the island to cut off the Patriots' retreat. Nearly a third of Washington's troops were in danger of being trapped and captured if the British could block their retreat.

Mary Lindley Murray
The Woman Who Stopped the British Army

THE BRITISH SHIPS KEPT COMING IN one after another along Kip's Bay by New York City. Mary Lindley Murray looked out of her upstairs bedroom window and watched as the longboats full of British soldiers landed. "There must be thousands of them," she thought. For Mary, a supporter of American independence, those British ships were disturbing.

Mary knew the Patriots were retreating from New York. Four thousand Patriot soldiers, with most of General Washington's supplies, were still nearby. The British soldiers could easily cut off their escape route. Mary knew the Americans would pass just a mile from her house. It might be hours before they reached safety. How could she protect those Patriot soldiers from the British army arriving on the longboats?

Then Mary had an idea. Her husband was loyal to the king and supported the British. The British officers arriving on the longboats would think it only natural if Mary invited them into her home for tea. "Beulah! Susan!" she called to her daughters. "Help the servants to get together our finest food and wine. We are inviting the British commanders to tea."

She told her daughters her plan to stall the British until the Patriot army had safely passed. Mary and her daughters put on their prettiest dresses. She then went into the kitchen and told a trusted maid of her plan. "Go upstairs and keep watch out the window. When you see the dust is no longer coming over the far trees, that will mean the Patriot soldiers have gotten past. Then come and offer to help me. I'll know I can then allow the British to leave."

Soon the British General came by leading his soldiers. The royal governor of New York was with him. "What a hot and dusty day this is," Mary said to the general. "Why don't you and the governor come in for tea?"

"We've got some Patriot rebels to catch," replied the general.

"Oh, those boys are long gone this morning," Mary lied. "We sure would like to show our appreciation for you driving them away. I know the governor is friends with my husband. My husband sure would be displeased with me if I wasn't hospitable to his friends."

Mary invited the general and his staff for tea.

"I really do appreciate your hospitality," the royal governor said, "but I'm worried about our troops waiting for us in the hot sun."

"No need to worry," Mary assured him. "I'll send food and drink out to them. They look tired and thirsty too." During tea Mary and her daughters laughed and spoke with their guests freely. All three charmed the British officers to keep them from catching the Patriots.

"We really must be going," said the British general.

"Oh, you can't," said Mary, who was still waiting for her maid to come downstairs. "You can't leave until you try some of my husband's fine wine."

"Oh, yes," her daughters insisted. The British stayed longer. As Mary was pouring more wine, her maid came into the room to see if she could help. From this signal Mary knew that the Patriots had safely passed. Relieved, Mary continued to be a gracious hostess.

"The Patriots are safe," she whispered to her daughters in the kitchen. "We have just saved General Washington's supplies and thousands of Patriot soldiers. Let's bid our wonderful guests good-bye." After the British had left, Mary told her daughters, "When your father returns from his trip, do not tell him about today."

By delaying the British for two hours, Mary and her daughters spoiled a chance for the British to capture 4,000 American prisoners. Mary Lindley Murray had stopped the British army.

Loyalists

Not everyone who lived in the colonies wanted to be independent from England. Many people were loyal to the king, and were called Loyalists or Tories. During the American Revolutionary War, many Loyalists moved to New York City while the British occupied it. After the war ended, thousands of Loyalists moved to Nova Scotia in Canada.

In 1780, the American Revolutionary War was in the fifth year, far longer than most people thought the war would last. The life of a Patriot soldier was difficult. Their farms and occupations were neglected. Morale suffered. Women were not expected to fight, yet they wanted to help.

Esther Reed

Organizer of the Philadelphia Association

"THE TIME HAS COME FOR THE WOMEN of Philadelphia to organize themselves and help our soldiers who are fighting in this war," said Esther Reed. She was speaking to several of her friends one day as they were sewing together.

"I agree," said her friend, Sarah Franklin Bache, who was Benjamin Franklin's daughter. "We know so many women, we could surely find some way to help."

"We can't go about it half-way, either," said Esther as she put down her needle and looked at all the women. "It has to be done right."

"Well," said Sarah, "I can't think of anyone better than you to do it." With this encouragement Esther started the Philadelphia Association which became the largest women's organization in the American Revolutionary War.

Esther's father was an English merchant who traded with the American colonies. Many young Americans came to visit their house in London. When Esther married an American in 1770, she moved to Philadelphia.

The Philadelphia Association sewed shirts for the Patriot soldiers.

Even though Esther was born and raised in England, she sided with her husband in the American fight for independence. Her husband was an aide to General Washington. Once the Declaration of Independence was signed and the fighting began, life became hard for Esther and other Patriots. It grew difficult to get basic items like food and clothing. Still Esther willingly relinquished the comforts of England to embrace her new country's cause.

After five years of fighting, Esther felt it was time for the women of Philadelphia to help General Washington's soldiers. "Let's do something for the Patriot soldiers," said Esther at the first meeting of the Philadelphia Association. "Those young men are in the fields fighting for us. We sit in our warm homes in winter while they freeze in their tents. They need our support."

Importance of Handicrafts

In colonial times, many products we buy, like shoes or bread, were made at home. Sewing was a skill taught to every girl as part of her education. Patriot women knitted and sewed homespun cloth into clothing to boycott British-made goods during the American Revolutionary War. Making cloth required carding and spinning to make wool, or soaking flax to spin it into linen. Women often joined together in sewing circles to talk while doing this work. The ability to sew tiny neat stitches was admired as a sign of domestic skill. If a woman became widowed, her skill as a seamstress could be used to earn money.

Esther's group, the Philadelphia Association, went from door to door to ask the citizens of Philadelphia for contributions. They were rarely turned down. Some women sold their jewelry to help. Servants gave money. The Philadelphia Association raised a large sum of money.

General Washington suggested the money go into the Patriot treasury. Esther wrote back a firm, 'No!" The women wanted to give the Patriot soldiers something special. When Esther offered to give the money directly to the soldiers, General Washington asked her not to. He feared the young men might waste it on drinking and gambling. Then General Washington recommended the money be used for high-quality warm shirts. The women of the Philadelphia Association agreed. To stretch their budget they bought the linen for the shirts and stitched over 2,000 shirts by hand.

Each woman put her name in the collar of each shirt she had sewn. The personal touch meant much to Patriot soldiers who sometimes felt forgotten. Esther Reed organized the women of Philadelphia to help the Patriot soldiers in a unique and special way. She reminded the men fighting in the American Revolutionary War how much they were appreciated.

Battle of Bennington

First Official Flag
of the United States

Gadsen-
Commander-in-Chief
of Continental Navy

Betsy Ross: Making the Flag

Betsy Ross is one of the best-known women of the American Revolution. She is credited with making the first American flag. Betsy was a Patriot whose first two husbands both died in the American Revolutionary War. The widow Betsy Ross was paid by the Pennsylvania State Navy Board in May 1777 for making "ship's colours, &c." These were flags used on boats for identification and signaling.

During the American Revolutionary War many different flags were used by the Patriots. These flags were made by individuals or local militias. The Continental Congress passed a Flag Resolution on June 14, 1777. The resolution said the flag should have thirteen red and white stripes and thirteen white stars on a blue field. The first record of Betsy Ross sewing the American flag appeared ninety years after the American Revolutionary War. In time her legend grew. No one knows for sure who really made the first American flag. The true origin and creator of the flag may forever stay a mystery. Maybe because of this, Betsy Ross's legend lives on.

United States flag today

Early in the American Revolutionary War, the Patriot army consisted of local militias. General Washington believed that the Patriots needed a professional full-time army to defeat the British. Washington wanted men for soldiers who would sign up for three years. One woman hid her identity and fought secretly and bravely as a Patriot soldier for a year and a half.

Deborah Sampson
Patriot Soldier Disguised as a Man

DEBORAH SAMPSON CUT HER HAIR, tied a cloth firmly around her chest and put on men's clothes. Walking all the way to Boston, she decided to travel even further. She wanted to go where no one could possibly know her. Deborah didn't want to be recognized because that might prevent her from joining the Patriot Army. When she reached Bellingham, Massachusetts, Deborah used her brother's name and enlisted in the 4th Massachusetts Regiment as a man.

Marching, fighting, and stalking the British soldiers by moonlight had sounded exciting to Deborah before she joined the Patriot army. She soon found out it was hard work in harsh conditions. Her wet boots left raw sores on her feet. The food was poor. And every day she had to make sure no one discovered her secret. To do this, she could only use the latrine in secret or take baths at night.

Still, fighting hard for her country was her goal. Deborah quickly gained the respect of her fellow soldiers. Once, during a battle with the British, she was wounded by a musket ball in her thigh. Not wanting her secret to be found out, she begged the other soldiers to let her die. They did not listen, but instead took her to a hospital. When she got there she convinced the surgeons to let her change her clothes alone. In private, keeping quiet to yet again protect her secret, she painfully extracted the musket ball from her own thigh.

Near the end of the American Revolutionary War, Deborah came down with a fever. While in the hospital she was so sick she could hardly move or make any sound to let anyone know she was alive. Dr. Barnabas Binney watched over her. He worried about the frail young boy who was his patient. While putting cold compresses on Deborah's chest, he saw where she had

Soldiers' Clothing

The British army wore red uniforms and thus were called redcoats. The Patriots often called them "Lobster Backs" as a put-down. The Patriot soldiers in the early years did not look like an army. Militias hadn't enough uniforms to go around. Soldiers wore whatever clothes they owned. In 1779, blue was made the official color of the Patriot uniforms. Even then, as cloth was in short supply, the Patriot soldiers had to make do with what they had.

bound her chest to hide her identity. Startled, the doctor looked around to see if anyone else had noticed. He was the only one in the room. He buttoned Deborah's shirt back quickly and quietly treated her. Later he took her to his own home to recover.

Dr. Binney kept Deborah's secret until after the war. When Deborah reported to West Point to complete her enlistment, the kindly doctor sent with her a letter to the commander. In the letter he explained how Deborah had kept her identity a secret while serving heroically in the army. On October 23, 1783, Deborah was honorably discharged from the Patriot Army.

Deborah still had to fight to receive her pension from Congress. Eventually Congress decided that the young girl who once cut her hair and used her brother's name to serve her country deserved as much credit as any man. When she died, her husband was the only man to receive a widower's pension from the American Revolutionary War.

◀ Dr. Binney kept Deborah's secret.

Many Native American tribes had no interest in which side won the American Revolutionary War. Both the British and Patriots wanted the Native Americans as allies. The British offered bribes to entice Native Americans into attacking Patriot settlers and outposts. The British hoped to keep frontiersmen busy and unable to join the Patriot army.

Nancy Ward
Beloved Woman of the Cherokee

TWENTY YEARS BEFORE THE AMERICAN REVOLUTIONARY WAR, during a battle with the Creek Indians, Nancy Ward saw her husband die. He was the chief and a great warrior. His death caused confusion and uncertainty amoung the Cherokees. Nancy had rushed into the fight and picked up his bow and arrow. She then led her tribe to victory.

Nancy had earned the name Agi-ga-u-e or "Beloved Women" of the Cherokee tribe because of this deed. This name was a title of recognition and importance. With it she became head of the Women's Council and also sat as a member of the Council of Chiefs. These were not mere honorary positions. In Cherokee society women owned the land and the wealth. It was passed from mother to daughter. When a couple married, the husband moved into the woman's house, and if they divorced, the man had to move out. Women had an equal say with men on war councils and treaty negotiations. The Women's Council could override decisions that men made. Leading the Women's Council was a great honor and a highly responsible position.

◀ Nancy led her tribe to victory.

Nancy Ward's given name was Nanye'hi but the white settlers called her Nancy. She befriended the Patriot settlers who came to her valley along the Tennessee River. Nancy always hoped her people would live in peace with them. When the British offered to pay Cherokee warriors to attack Patriot settlers, she ran to tell her friend, John Sevier. Arriving at his house, she was out of breath.

Cherokee Life

The Cherokees lived in permanent towns. Each town had 30-60 log cabins built around a large central meeting hall. Women grew crops and provided the majority of the food, while men hunted. In the central meeting hall special occasions like weddings and funerals were held. All the important decisions were made there too. With priests, chiefs, elders and beloved women leading the discussions, the Cherokees' goal for tribal harmony rested on everyone agreeing to important decisions. If one person disagreed with the whole town, they might be banned and sent away.

With many white settlers moving into Cherokee territory in the 1770's, tribal harmony broke down as younger warriors chose to fight while many elders sought peace. Disharmonies grew so great that the war party of the Cherokees left to form their own tribe called the Chickamaugus. In the end, the settlers would take over all their land.

"What is the matter, Nancy?" John asked as he opened the door and saw her worried face.

"There's going to be an attack," she said, breathing hard. "It is going to be soon. I overheard some of the men talking." John helped Nancy into his house and offered her a drink of water.

"What type of attack are they planning?" he asked.

"Some Cherokees will attack those of you who are not loyal to the British king. The British are offering rewards to warriors who will fight," she answered. Then she drank deeply. "I really must get back," she said standing up. "I don't want anyone to know that I have come here to talk to you."

"Thank you, Nancy," John said as he walked her to the door. "I'll tell everyone and we'll be prepared." The Patriot settlers turned back the Cherokee attack because of Nancy's warning. They punished the warriors who fought for the British by destroying Cherokee settlements, but those of Nancy's Chota clan were left untouched.

In 1780, Nancy once again warned the Patriot settlers about another attack. When the settlers organized themselves for the battle, Nancy went to them and tried to find some way the two sides could compromise. When she failed, the Patriot settlers destroyed more Cherokee towns. When the two sides met after the battle Nancy once again urged a compromise between the Cherokee and the Patriot settlers. She spoke eloquently for a "chain of friendship" between the two groups. Nancy was a main voice when the Treaty of Hopewell was signed in 1785.

Nancy's hope that the native people and the settlers would learn to live with each other in peace never left her. She died in 1822 and was buried in the Tennessee hills she loved.

In the 1770's, the idea of open rebellion against the king grew, but not fast enough for some people. Mercy Otis Warren is one person whose anonymous writings fanned the flames of liberty and swayed thousands of people to the Patriot cause.

Mercy Otis Warren
Patriot Playwright

MERCY OTIS WARREN HAD TWELVE BROTHERS AND SISTERS. Her father held the unconventional view that education was as important for his daughters as it was for his sons. After Mercy married, she spent her spare time reading about history and politics. The more she learned about how the British were treating the American colonies, the madder she became.

Mercy's husband was a member of the Massachusetts legislature. Many political meetings were held at their house and Mercy stayed well-informed. In 1772, the first Committee of Correspondence was started in the Warren home. Within a year, seventy-five other committees spread around the colonies. Through these committees the Patriots throughout the colonies kept each other informed and shared revolutionary ideas.

Mercy's many letters were full of anger towards the British. She was an avid supportor of the Patriot cause. Though she spent time corresponding with famous Patriots, she felt it was more important to reach out to the common people. What could be done to get revolutionary ideas out to the public? Mercy asked John Adams how she could help spread the idea of freedom.

In her playwrighting, Mercy made fun of the British. ▶

Adams was impressed with Mercy's writing. He agreed with her that the common man and woman needed to be inspired for the cause of freedom. He suggested she write something funny about the British that would appeal to the public. She took his suggestion and wrote a play. In her first play, Mercy Warren made fun of the British military.

Her play could not be performed in Massachusetts because the Puritans who had founded the colony disapproved of plays as undignified and anti-religious. Their laws forbidding the performance of plays were still in effect. The British authorities also would not permit any public gathering that encouraged revolution. So Mercy's play was published in a magazine. People read the play like a story.

Mercy's first play was a hit. By making fun of the British, she had struck a popular chord with the colonists. Mercy did not tell anyone she was the author. The British could punish those who made fun of how they were handling the colonists. They might even put her in jail if they found out Mercy had written it.

Mercy published three more plays, all anonymously, before the American Revolutionary War broke out. They were so popular some were printed as separate booklets and sold in all thirteen colonies. As her plays became famous among the colonists, she was having second thoughts about her writing career.

Mercy wrote to John Adams. She feared her writings might bring scandal on her. Adams wrote Mercy's husband, urging him to convince her to keep

Books in Colonial America

Many colonial Americans had a Bible and a *Farmer's Almanac.* Books, though expensive, were popular enough to support over fifty bookstores by 1776. Being well-read was a sign of breeding. Most books were printed in England. American interests ranged from the Greek and Roman classics to Voltaire's philosophy to the popular *Robinson Crusoe.* The few public libraries that existed all charged a yearly fee and the books could not be checked out. Colonists had to read the books at the library.

writing. "God Almighty has entrusted her with powers for the good of the world, which . . . he bestows on few of the human race. Instead of being a fault to use them, it would be criminal to neglect them."

Once the fighting started, Mercy's husband commanded Patriot ships attacking the British navy. Since this work kept him away from home, Mercy decided to work on a history of the American Revolutionary War starting back in the 1760's. Using the notes she had kept during meetings and conversations, she began what turned into a thirty-year project. Her three-volume history was published in 1805 and titled *History of the Rise, Progress, and Termination of the American Revolution.*

Before the American Revolutionary War, only a few Patriot leaders knew what a great talent Mercy had. After the final American victory, Mercy was able to take credit for her writings. She was one of the most influential writers of her time.

Brought to America as a slave, Phillis Wheatley exhibited great intelligence and poise. She became a Patriot and later a symbol for abolitionists pressing for African-American slaves to be set free.

Phillis Wheatley
The First African-American Author

BY THE TIME PHILLIS WAS SEVEN YEARS OLD, she had been captured, transported to the America colonies and sold as a slave. Though she tried to push it out of her mind, she still had memories of being taken from her family. How she had cried while she was being put on the slave ship!

When the ship reached Boston, a family called Wheatley bought Phillis. The Wheatleys named her Phillis after the ship that brought her to America. They noticed Phillis's inquisitive nature and intelligence and decided to treat her very differently from most slaves. They gave Phillis her own room and had her eat with the family. The Wheatley children taught Phillis how to read and write.

"Now this is how we spell 'summer'," the children said, writing the letters out slowly so Phillis could hear the sounds. Phillis concentrated hard while biting her lip and listening to the sound of each letter. They sounded so beautiful to her ears, "s-u-m-m-e-r." She loved the way they flowed together and brought to her mind pictures of green grass and warm days. That's what

◀ Phillis read her poem to General Washington.

Slavery During the Revolution

By 1776, black slaves made up approximately 20% of the population in the American colonies. Most slaves entered America demoralized after being kidnapped, packed into filthy slave ships, sold and branded. Few were Christian at the time of the American Revolution, as many colonists did not believe slaves had souls to be saved. In 1774, the New England colonies banned slave trading, the beginning of the abolitionist movement that freed the slaves ninety years later.

words were to her, pictures in her mind. It wasn't long before she started putting words together in poems and realized how wonderful it made her feel to share them with others.

Phillis certainly was smart. Within sixteen months of arriving in America, she could speak perfect English. She could read and write. She understood even difficult passages of the Bible. Impressed with her talents, the Wheatleys encouraged Phillis to read her poetry in public. Phillis became a local celebrity. That was unusual for any woman in colonial America, and much more unusual for a woman from Africa.

Phillis's first published poem appeared on Dec. 21, 1767 in the Newport, Rhode Island newspaper. Phillis's poems celebrated learning and virtue, spoke of the saving power of Jesus, and described a yearning for freedom. She wrote a number of patriotic poems on subjects like the Boston Massacre, Patriot generals, America's greatness, and the peace treaty of 1783 that ended the American Revolutionary War. Her most famous was a poem to George Washington. She was the earliest person to refer to him as "first in peace."

Washington enjoyed Phillis's poem so much that he asked to meet her. Phillis, who had been brought to America on a slave ship, spent a private hour talking with the leader of the Patriot Army. The poem was published several times during the American Revolutionary War to promote the Patriot cause.

Phillis went to England when she was a teenager. There she met the Countess of Huntingdon, who was so impressed with Phillis's poems that she financed Phillis's only book, *Poems on Various Subjects, Religious and Moral*. Eighteen prominent Bostonians certified in the forward that Phillis was the genuine author.

In 1778, after the Wheatley parents and children had all passed away or left the colonies, Phillis was given her freedom. Phillis then addressed the issue of freedom in her writings. She called both for the need of freedom from England and from slavery. "In every human Breast, God has implanted a Principle, which we call Love of Freedom; it is impatient of Oppression, and pants for Deliverance," she wrote.

Phillis Wheatley was America's first published black author. A Patriot and later a symbol for the abolition of slavery, she will always be known as a contributor to freedom.

In war it always helps to have advance knowledge of the enemy's intentions. During the American Revolutionary War, the Patriots had an American spy in the heart of King George's court.

Patience Wright

American Spy in King George's Court

WHEN PATIENCE WRIGHT'S HUSBAND DIED before the American Revolutionary War began, he left Patience with five children. Patience had to find a way to support her family and decided to try her skill at molding wax into human sculptures. Wax sculpture was a popular art form in colonial America. Most wax artists made statues of historical figures. Patience chose to concentrate her work on living subjects. Her excellent artistic skill made her famous.

Her talent was sought out by wealthy patrons. The figures she made were so life-like they were sometimes mistaken for real people. Abigail Adams tells how she watched a minister reading a newspaper in Patience's studio for several minutes before realizing he was made of wax! Patience sold her statues for a lot of money. But she lost everything when a fire destroyed her New York studio. She then decided to move to London, England where her friend, Benjamin Franklin, was living.

The English at this time were drawn by the "natural and simple" style of the American colonists. Patience combined those qualities with an eccentric

Patience learned important information from her patrons. ▶

and charming personality. When Benjamin Franklin introduced her to London society, people asked her to make their statues in wax. Word of her talent reached King George III who invited her to Buckingham Palace, where the king and queen posed for her. The royal couple accepted this eccentric artist from the "American wilderness" with good humor. They even smiled when Patience insisted on addressing them as George and Charlotte instead of by their royal titles.

Even after Patience had been accepted into British society she remained loyal to her "dear America," as she called it. When trouble started back home, Patience decided she could help America's fight for independence from her art studio in London. Her patrons were used to talking freely around her. While they posed, Patience would bring the conversation around to the rebellion in the colonies. When Patience heard a new general was going to America, she always found a reason to invite his nearest relative for a sitting. In this way she learned important information, like the number of the general's troops and their exact destination in America.

Spies

Both sides used spies during the American Revolutionary War. Paul Revere was head of a spy ring called the Mechanics. Besides warning the minutemen that the British were coming, his spies stole cannons and gunpowder from the British on numerous occassions. One of his mechanics, Dr. Benjamin Church, was also spying for the British!

The best known Patriot spy was Nathan Hale. The British captured him and before his hanging he is reported to have said, "I regret that I have but one life to give for my country."

Getting her intelligence back to the colonies proved simple. She hid the messages inside wax figures which she sent to museums in America. John Hancock is quoted as complimenting her efforts as a spy. Patience's business in London suffered as the American Revolutionary War progressed. She became known as a supporter in the rebellion against King George III. Her friend Benjamin Franklin moved to France as the American ambassador. Still Patience stayed on in England.

A few Englishmen were sympathetic to the American cause. They helped American sailors imprisoned in England to escape from jail. Patience often sheltered these fleeing prisoners at her house while they were on their escape route. Patience eventually became homesick and dreamed of returning to America. She wrote that she could not be "content to have her bones laid in London." Patience didn't have a choice in the matter. She suffered from a bad fall and died in London in 1786. She was buried there.

There is one known piece of her work still in existence. At Westminster Abbey is a full-length figure of William Pitt, the Earl of Chatham. This is a fitting legacy for Patience, since Lord Pitt was the English member of parliament most supportive of the colonies' demands before the American Revolutionary War.

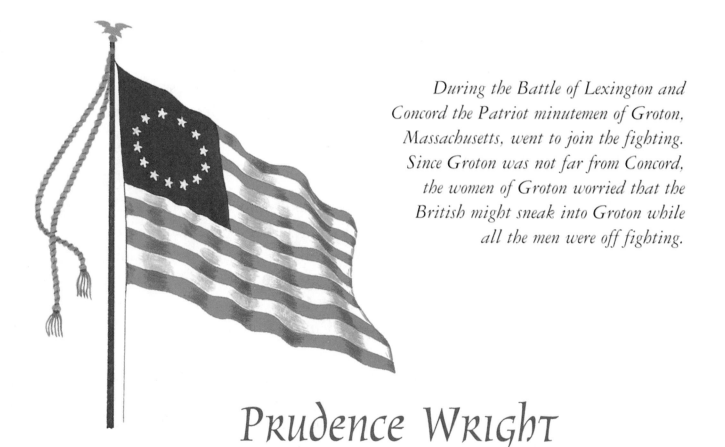

During the Battle of Lexington and Concord the Patriot minutemen of Groton, Massachusetts, went to join the fighting. Since Groton was not far from Concord, the women of Groton worried that the British might sneak into Groton while all the men were off fighting.

Prudence Wright
Commander of the Minutewomen

AS THE ALARM SOUNDED THROUGH THE TOWN OF GROTON, Prudence Wright watched her husband prepare to fight the British. "We knew they were coming," her husband said as he pulled on his boots and checked one of his muskets. "We just didn't know when."

Prudence knew that all over town men were preparing to defend their Massachusetts town against the British. As her husband put on his coat he said, "All of you women please stay in one place. There could be trouble." He got on his horse and rode away. Prudence knew she had no time to waste. Only the women of the town were left to stop any British from crossing Jewett's Bridge. If the British were going to sneak into Groton, they would have to cross the bridge.

Prudence ran to her friend's houses and asked for help in gathering the women of the town. "Tell them to wear their husbands' clothing! Bring whatever weapons are left! Muskets, if there are any, pitchforks if they have to," she told them.

It wasn't long before a group of women dressed in their husbands' clothing gathered in the front room of Prudence's house. Prudence looked around at the group. It was hard to recognize them dressed liked men. She was so used to seeing them in long skirts or dresses. "We must look a sight," she thought as she tucked her hair into her husband's hat. "Ladies," she said, holding up her hand to get their attention. "We must act fast. We are going to Jewett's Bridge and defend it from the British."

The women cheered as they heard her words. "No British will cross over that bridge tonight. Not with us defending it." With those words, Prudence led the group out into the night. No one spoke as they silently walked through fields and woods. All anyone could hear was the occasional night owl and the sound of their feet quietly crunching the ground.

"We'll make sure that these secret messages
get to the local Patriot committee."

Colonial Clothing

Young colonial boys and girls dressed alike. They wore long dresses with underskirts called petticoats. At about six years of age, they began wearing adult clothes.

Women wore long skirts with petticoats underneath. Around their waists they wore a wide belt called a corset. Thin pieces of whale bone were sewn into the corsets, forcing women to stand erect. The corset was tied tightly, making breathing difficult. Women wore little hankerchiefs called clouts on their heads. In cold weather, they wore wool cloaks.

Men wore knee breeches instead of pants. Breeches came down just over the knees. They were made of leather. The front and back were the same so that the breeches could be worn either way. This kept the knees and seat from wearing out too fast.

Men wore linen shirts, with a sleeveless jacket called a waistcoat over them. On Sundays, men would put a jacket on over the waistcoat. Knit stockings tied with cord came up to the knees.

All the colonists followed the latest fashions from London. Rich men wore powdered white wigs, just like English gentlemen. Women changed their styles each year in dresses and hair designs.

Arriving at the bridge, they hid among the bushes, crouching down so no one approaching could see them. "If we have to, we will stay here all night," Prudence told the group. They all agreed and took their places. After what seemed an eternity of straining to hear an approaching enemy, they definitely heard the sound of horse hooves on the wooden bridge. The women had agreed among themselves that Prudence would make the sound of an owl as the signal for them to spring the ambush.

When she gave the signal the women sprang from cover and quickly surrounded a British captain. The captain was too startled to try to escape. In the dark he didn't realize at first that his captors were women. "Don't think you can get away from us," Prudence told him in a low voice so he would think she was a man. She held a pitchfork up in his face. He listened to her carefully.

"Let's take him to the stockade," said one woman as she tied his hands behind him.

"First, let's see if he has any hidden messages," said another, removing his boots. As she pulled them off, several sheets of paper slipped out and fell to the ground.

"Secret messages," said Prudence. "We'll make sure that they get to the local Patriot Committee of Safety."

Later that evening when they were changing back into their clothes, the women laughed at how surprised the British officer had been to be ambushed at the bridge. "Did you see how shocked he was when he realized we were a group of farmers' wives who just happened to be wearing our husbands' clothes?" asked one woman.

"The British must learn not only to fight the men but also the women of the colonies," said Prudence, as she took off her husband's hat and put on her own. "Liberty is just as important to us women as it is to our men."

On the frontier, danger might come any time. Twice during the American Revolutionary War, Fort Henry was attacked by British-led Indians. Wheeling, West Virginia, was considered part of Virginia during the period of the American Revolutionary War.

Elizabeth Zane
The Heroine of Fort Henry

ELIZABETH ZANE PAUSED FROM HER WORK long enough to stretch the ache out of her back. The bright sun made her forget the early autumn chill in the mountain air. Now, looking around the valley of the Ohio River, she thought, "It is so beautiful here, it is hard to believe how difficult this past year has been."

Elizabeth, who was sixteen, lived with her brother just outside Fort Henry, near Wheeling in present-day West Virginia. The fort was named in honor of Patrick Henry. Life on the western Virginia frontier had become increasingly dangerous as the American Revolutionary War dragged on. Indian tribes, encouraged and armed by the British, attacked such outposts. The Zanes' house had been burned down the year before. It had taken them most of a year to rebuild it. Even though the house was close to the fort, the Zanes stockpiled gunpowder in it as a precaution.

As Elizabeth was hanging clothes out in the fresh air, she heard screams coming from beyond the edge of the woods. Rushing back to the house she

Elizabeth ran back to the fort with the gunpowder. ▶

Children in Revolutionary America

Children had less play time in the 1700's. Work was thought to build character and there was plenty to do. Many products from clothes to tools were home-made and children learned crafts early. Boys became apprentices to learn a trade if they lived in a town. Girls were taught at home. Children wore clothes similiar to adults. Boys joined the militia at sixteen and most girls were married by seventeen or eighteen.

Most children were educated at home, not at school. Still there were close to one hundred schools around Philadelphia in the 1770's and plenty in New England. Few girls attended schools. The school year was shorter and the family farming needs came first. Students had to sometimes make their own ink from soot and water and bring it to school. Penmanship was considered very important but spelling was not, which led to some very creative spelling. Paper was costly and poorer students might practice their penmanship on birch bark.

ran into her brother. "Get to the fort! Get to the fort!" he shouted at her. "The Indians are attacking." Hurrying beside her brother to the fort, Elizabeth dropped the clothes she had not yet hung on the clothesline.

Once inside the fort, Elizabeth helped the other women gather weapons and load the guns. The women also brought in buckets of water from the well to put out fires and quench the soldier's thirst. The fighting between the Patriot settlers and the British-led Indians lasted two full days. By then, only twelve of the forty-two men were still standing. The settlers were running out of gunpowder. Elizabeth knew that there was no way they could keep fighting without gunpowder. "We have gunpowder back at my house," Elizabeth's brother yelled.

"One of you men will have to run to his house to get some," shouted the leader of the fort. Several men raised their hands to volunteer, but Elizabeth knew what she had to do. "You have not one man to spare," she said bravely. "I know where the gunpowder is in my brother's house. I'll go get it."

"Be careful," her brother said as she ran out of the fort. Arrows and bullets flew around her. Then an amazing thing happened! As soon as the Indians saw her, they shouted "Squaw! Squaw!" and held their fire.

As Elizabeth shut the door to the house, she caught her breath for just a second. Then she emptied a keg of gunpowder into a tablecloth and tied it around her waist. "I'm not going to be able to run back as fast," she thought as she stood at the doorway. Taking a deep breath she opened the door and started back. Now the Indians realized Elizabeth was carrying gunpowder back to the fort. This time they showed no mercy to her. Shots rang around her head. She felt an arrow whiz past. Elizabeth knew she had almost been hit.

Finally reaching the fort, she ran through the gate. Her brother was there to meet her and to untie the tablecloth from around her waist. Flushed, Elizabeth looked down at her skirt and saw a huge hole where a musket ball had gone straight through it.

"Thank goodness I made it back," she said.

"You were so brave," the other women said, gathering around. One brought her some water to drink.

"I just hope we can save our fort," said Elizabeth after she took a long drink.

The next day Patriot soldiers arrived and drove off the attackers. The gunpowder Elizabeth had brought back was enough to hold off the Indians and save Fort Henry. Elizabeth has long been remembered for her bravery. One hundred and fifty years after her act of courage, a statue commemorating her bravery was built beside her grave in Martin's Ferry, Ohio.

Index

Abigail Adams, 8, 9-11, 78
Adams, John, 9, 10, 11, 70
African-American author, first, 75-77
American Revolutionary War Events, 6
Arnett, Hannah, 12-14
Asbury, Mrs., 16, 17

Bache, Sarah Franklin, 59
Barker, Penelope, 15-17
Barry, Catherine Moore, 18-19
beds in colonial times, 34
Bellingham, Massachusetts, 61
Binney, Dr. Barnabas, 64, 65
books in colonial America, 72
Boston, Massachusetts, 10, 17, 63, 75
Boston Massacre, 76
Braintree, Massachusetts, 10
Bratton, Martha, 20-23
British, 15, 16, 18, 19, 20, 22, 23, 25, 26,
        27, 29, 30, 31, 32-34, 36-38, 39-41, 42-44,
        45-48, 49, 51, 53-55, 56-58, 63, 67, 68,
        70, 72, 73, 80, 82, 83, 85
Broad River, South Carolina, 36
Bunker Hill, battle of, 11
Burgin, Elizabeth, 24-27

cannons, 29, 30, 51
camp followers, 29, 30
Charlestown, South Carolina, 20, 53
Cherokees:
        Council of Chiefs, 69
        life of the, 68
        territory, 68, 69
        Women's Council, 67
Chickamaugas, 68
children of the 1770's, 88
clothing, colonial, 84
clothing, soldiers, 65
Committee of Correspondence, 70
Concord, Massachusetts, 82
Continental Congress, 9, 10, 25, 27, 31, 62
Corbin, John, 29, 30, 31

Corbin, Margaret, 28-31
Cornwallis, General, 18
Countess of Huntingdon, 77
Cowpens, South Carolina, 18, 19
Creek Indians, 67

Danbury, Connecticut, 42
Darragh, Lydia, 32-35
Declaration of Allegiance, 12
Declaration of Independence, 15, 60
Dooley, Colonel, 41

Edenton, North Carolina, 15
Edenton Tea Party, 15, 17
Elizabethtown, New Jersey, 12
England, 10, 11

fire arrows, 54, 55
flag, making the, 62
Flag Resolution, 62
Fort Henry, 86, 89
Fort Lee, 12
Fort Motte, 55
Fort Washington, 29, 31
Franklin, Benjamin, 59, 78, 79, 80
Fredericksburg, New York, 41

Geiger, Emily, 36-38
Georgia, 39, 41
Greene, General Nathaniel, 36, 37, 38, 45
Groton, Massachusetts, 82
gunpowder, 10, 20, 21, 22, 86-89

Hale, Nathan, 80
Hancock, John, 80
Hart, Nancy, 39-41
History of the Rise, Progress and Termination
        of the American Revolution, 73
Hudson River, 12

Invalid Regiment, 31

King, Elizabeth, 17
King George III, 78, 80

letters, (mail in colonial times), 11
Liberty Boys, 41
London, England, 78, 79, 80, 81
Long Island Sound, 44
Loyalists (Tories), 58
Ludington, Colonel, 42,44
Ludington, Sybil, 42-44

marriage in the 1770's, 47
Martin, Grace, 45-48
Martin, Rachel, 45-48
Martin's Ferry, Ohio, 89
McCauley, John 49, 51
McCauley, Molly Hays (Molly Pitcher), 49-52
minutemen, 82
minutewomen, 82
Monmouth, New Jerseey, 49
Morgan, General, 18, 19
Motte, Rebecca, 53-55
Murray, Mary Lindley, 56-58

Native Americans, 67
New England, 88
New York City, New York, 12, 29, 56
Newport, Rhode Island, 76
newspapers, colonial, 14

Patriot army (also Contintental army,
    Washington's army), 12, 13, 18, 19, 20,
    23, 24, 25, 26, 27, 29, 30, 31, 32-35,
    36-38, 39-41, 42, 43, 44, 45, 49-52, 56-
    58, 59-61, 62, 63-65, 67, 77, 78, 82, 86,
    89
Patriot Committee of Safety, 85
peace treaty, 15, 8
Pennsylvania, State of, 52,62
pension, 31, 52, 65
Philadelphia, 9, 31, 32, 34, 59, 88
Philadelphia Association, 59, 60, 61
Pitt, Lord William, 80
Poems on Various Subjects, Religious and Moral, 77
prison ships, 24, 25
prisoners, 24, 25, 26
Puritans, 72

Quakers, (also Society of Friends) 32
Queen Charlotte, 80

Reed, Esther, 59-61
Regiment, 4th Massachusetts, 63
Revere, Paul, 42, 44, 80
Ridgefield, Connecticut, 44
Ross, Betsy, 62

Sampson, Deborah, 63-65
sculpture, wax, 78, 80, 81
Sevier, John, 68-69
slavery, 10, 11, 75, 76
spies, 80
Sumter, General Thomas, 36, 37, 38

taxes, 17
tea, 15, 17
Tennessee, 39
travel in the 1770's, 38
Treaty of Hopewell, 69

Ward, Nancy, 66-69
Warren Mercy Otis, 10, 70-73
Washington, General George:
    army, 12, 13, 32, 51, 52, 60,, 61, 63
    Continental Congress, 25
    Elizabeth Burgin's letter to, 27
    "first in peace," 71
    horse, 49
    Phillis Wheatley poem to, 74-75, 76
    Whitemarsh, camp at, 34, 35
    Yorktown, 18
Wateree River, 36
Westminster Abbey, 80
Whitemarsh, Pennsylvania, 32, 35
Wheatley, Phillis, 74-77
Wheatley family, 75, 76, 77
Wheeling, West Virginia, 86
Women's inequality, 9
Wright, Patience, 78-81
Wright, Prudence, 82-85

Yorktown, Virginia, 18

Zane, Elizabeth, 88-91

About the Author

Heroines of the American Revolution: America's Founding Mothers is Diane Silcox-Jarrett's third book. She wrote *One Woman's Dream*, a biography of African-American educator Charlotte Hawkins Brown and co-authored the autobiography of the National Basketball Association player, Reggie Williams

Diane Silcox-Jarrett has taught creative writing and has been writer-in-residence for schools in Raleigh and Wake County of North Carolina. She has been a radio news director, an editor, and speech writer for North Carolina state officials. She is a graduate of Elon College.

Diane lives near Raleigh, North Carolina, with her husband Alex and their children Daniel and Kimberly.

About the Artist

Art Seiden is a prizewinning illustrator of over 100 children's books He has been engaged as an illustrator by most of the leading publishers and corporations of the United States.

Art is a painter who has exhibited extensively. His favorite medium is watercolor and favorite subject is early-Americana. He was a fine arts major and graduated with degrees from Queens College and Pratt Institute.

Art resides in Woodmere, New York, with his wife, Bea, who is also an artist.